The Kite Of Your Genius ... Lifts Your Community

ANTHROPOSOPHICAL PUBLICATIONS
FREMONT, MICHIGAN USA

THE KITE OF YOUR GENIUS ... LIFTS YOUR COMMUNITY
By Jean W. Yeager

© 2020 Jean W. Yeager
Lucky Phone Call Publishing
38 Kendall Ave., Rutland, VT 05701

Some of these chapters appeared as bLog posts on
https://www.threesimplequestions.blogspot.com/

The title and lead essay, "THE KITE OF YOUR GENIUS" was the winner in the 2016 Ageless Authors (age 65+) National Essay Competition

Anthroposophical Publications has no responsibility for the persistence or accuracy of URLs for external or third-party Internet Websites referred to in this publication and does not guarantee that any content on such Websites is, or will remain, accurate or appropriate.

Edited by:
James D. Stewart
https://www.elib.com/

Published by
Anthroposophical Publications
Fremont, Michigan US
https://AnthroposophicalPublications.org/

ISBN: 978-1-948302-59-3 paperback
978-1-948302-60-9 eBook

Very Short Essays and Intense Creative Non-Fiction

With Loft by Rudolf Steiner's "Facing Karma"
Mixed with Lyrics by Dylan, Simon, Marley, & More
"Awakening To Community," "New Faithfulness"

by
Jean W. Yeager

Award Winning Essayist, Playwright, Prison Volunteer, Waldorf Dad, Quaker, Former Administrative Director of The Anthroposophical Society in America

TABLE OF CONTENTS

1) ABOUT THIS COLLECTION VII

2) KITE OF YOUR GENIUS – "In kite making, you have to add tension to have enough arc to generate lift." 1

3) FROM NAÏVE IDEALISM TO ACHIEVED IDEALISM – "We meet our true capacities in this tussle over idealism." 7

4) I AM YOUR NESTED SYSTEM – *"Lend me your Higher Self, will ya?"* 11

5) YOU AND WILLIAM SHAKESPEARE DREAM ONE ANOTHER – "We are all sleepers in the dreams of others. Before you were born, lofty spiritual beings dreamed you into existence." 15

6) I AM YOUR CRISIS – "I want to live, and love, in universal imperfection. Couch surf with your karmic carpool." 19

7) LET'S REVERSE OUR WILL, SHALL WE? – THE STRUGGLE FOR THE NEW FAITHFULNESS – "Here are the things which you can't control." · 21

8) AGE 28-35: THE WISER PERSON WITHIN US – "Yoohoo! Someone is leading the change." 25

9) REMIX – *"FACING KARMA"* – Steiner lecture excerpts REMIXED and contemporary rock lyrics: Paul Simon, Bob Dylan, Bob Marley, Bruce Springsteen, and more. 29

10) DEVOTION BECOMES SACRIFICE – "Self-sacrifice is terribly uncomfortable, just ask the seed." 39

11) THE SUBSTANCE OF LOVE – "My Auntie Helen transformed the 'Instance Rice' into the Substance of Love." 41

12) SELECTING OMENS – "The spiritual world relies on we humans to be responsible for life in the material world." ······················ 45

13) REPORT OF TEACHING RUDOLF STEINER'S SIX SUBSIDIARY EXERCISES IN MY LOCAL JAIL – Simple as that. ······························· 47

14) SHE COAXES THE HUMAN SPIRIT – "Agonizingly, slowly she can hear the heart creaking open …" ································ 53

15) ARDUOUS — BESCHWERLICH ARDU — И ВЗРЫВООПАСНЫХ —مشكل – "I HOPE THIS IS AN ARDUOUS OR TOUGH TIME FOR YOU." ····················· 55

16) WHO LETS THE DOGS OUT? – I keep three big dogs: Anger, Doubt and Hate. ··· 57

17) I AM DISINCARNATION - AGE 42 – "The gradual grapevine dance step off the stage of life." ································ 59

18) PINBALL AGE – "I am now propelled by the gravity of aging and the inertia of my vanities." ································ 61

19) CALL TO ACTION – "The Kite Of Your Genius Lifts Your Community" The Genius Of The Communities Lifts The Society. ············· 65

20) ABOUT THE AUTHOR, JEAN W. YEAGER ······························ 67

21) OTHER BOOKS BY JEAN W. YEAGER ································· 71

About This Collection

IT'S SIMPLE, REALLY.

We are like kites. The vertical stick of the kite of our Genius runs between yourself and the spiritual world where you get your inspirations and insights. The horizontal stick runs between us to our family and community.

We bend or arc these sticks through our efforts or experiences so that our kite cannot just survive in the headwinds of life but gain lift and rise up. We can fine-tune the airfoil of our lives to withstand even greater headwinds.

The secret is that the kite of you, of your Genius, is connected with many others — friends, family, or workplace. When you rise, you lift them, too.

How does this book help?

The question for many of us is, what is it that that gives us lift? Or why am I spinning out of control? Or feeling dragged down with no lift? The key to self-understanding is to take a brief moment of reflection.

Each chapter in this book offers you the opportunity to read one or another of the short essays or intense creative nonfiction pieces (meaning "quick reads"). They are about the struggles of life. They may be different than your life, but considering each by contrast or comparison changes your thinking and offers a very brief moment of clarity.

They are not about fantasy, fiction, romance; they are about your life.

There is no set order, and you can return to any one of the other any time you wish.

It is as simple as that. Sail on!

THE KITE OF YOUR GENIUS

2016 WINNER AGELESS AUTHORS (AGE 65+) NATIONAL ESSAY COMPETITION, https://www.agelessauthors.com/

AGE 12 WAS ONE OF THOSE tension-filled crossing points in my life. It was a time when the tenderness and lack of confidence in childhood were waning, and I was beginning to test my growing body, to create my intellect. My *Genius* arrived in a pre-teenage "do-it-yourself kit."

There never are any specific instructions. All early teens or preteens struggle to form our "self." We wrestle with this unique, "higher self" and meet or create all kinds of challenges, inner and outer, large and small. *Our* gifts seem to emerge from our engagement in our conflict with, or our fleeing from authority.

In 1960, my family lived in a particularly windy part of Colorado just east of the Rocky Mountains out on the prairies in a bedroom community named Broomfield between Boulder and Denver. The wind blew so hard out there that the metallic threshold on our front door vibrated and hummed loudly whenever the wind velocity topped 40 miles an hour, which was frequently, at all hours of day or night.

My mother had been a young woman in the "Dirty 30s" in Iowa and Texas. That was the era of drought and giant clouds of dust that would blow up, become storms, and roll across the open prairies engulfing farms and lives. So, she knew the tragedy borne by ill winds of the Great Depression and World War II.

Age 12, for me, was also *the* age of grandeur. Grand ideas, climbing physical or metaphorical mountains, taking on significant challenges, seemed just the thing for learning about the truth of life, what is behind the scenes.

In my case, life gave us wind, lots of wind, and we foolhardy boys seeking a thrill made "bike boats." "Bike boats" were a way for us to test ourselves, our creativity, and find grand adventure.

Two kids would ask our mothers for an old, worn-out bedsheet and getting on our bikes, hold the sheet between us, so it caught the wind like a sail and propelled us. We would ride our bicycles holding the sheet with hands *off* the handlebars rocketing down dirt farm roads, whooping and hollering.

When we crashed, and we *did* crash, we got the misery we apparently wanted to experience. The world, life, gave us feedback on our "great and adventuresome ideas." We would limp home, trying not to cry, practicing swear words aimed at the wind, dragging along our busted bikes, sprains and bruises and composing great lies about our adventures and daring one another for our next even grander exploit.

My father was shocked by this risky behavior and my lack of sound judgment. I was a mild-mannered only child, never before prone to such risk-taking. My actions were new and disconcerting. You see, I was adopted at birth, so to have a small child from different parents, and you would expect you may see "genetic differences," even mental abilities. But, when that child grows to preteen-hood, teenage-ness, and you see personality traits that are radically different from yours, you wonder, "who is this person who is doing these risky things?"

Had I been my Dad's genetic son, he could've understood that my behavior may have somehow been somewhere in the "family tree." My father had a "disobedient" brother, my Uncle Stan, so if we were genetically linked, he could understand how the son of "good" Winston could be so rebellious, "Aw, he's like his Uncle!"

My Dad told a story about his brother, my Uncle Stan. Their father was a Methodist minister in small towns in Iowa. On Communion Sundays, he would say "come by the center aisle and leave by the side," which my father dutifully obeyed when it was his turn. My uncle, on the other hand, would go forward dancing up a side aisle and, when done with Communion, would turn with a flourish and caper down the center aisle back to his seat."

With "Bike Boats," my father could tell that his son was changing – and maybe not in such a positive way.

He may have saved me from further damage when he gave me one of the best, yet perhaps a most modest gift that a father could ever give a boy aged 12 – a bundle of raw, balsa wood kite sticks.

"Look what I found at the Army surplus store!" he said with sparkling eyes as he physically radiated joy!

There must have been 100 pre-made sets of kite sticks without the cheap paper covering that was typically found in that era's 10-cent drugstore kites. A broken kite stick was less threatening than a broken limb. So, for the next several weeks, while our bruises healed, my friends and I (and my Dad) made kites, *dozens* of kites of all configurations. We *became* kites.

• • • •

THE GREATER THE HEADWIND challenge of the life of a young person, the higher the potential to rise. Twelve-year-old's are the *holy boy (sanctus puer)* or the *holy girl (sancta puella)*, the Genius we ride in our lives to grandeur is the kite of our selves.

My "headwinds" were nothing compared to those of such people as a homeless black girl named Ella Fitzgerald, who transformed her neighborhood talent contest into the launchpad for a lifetime singing career. Slavery, neglect, and horrific abuse spun George Washington Carver into the heights of scientific discovery.

Genius will work with whatever it has at hand to fashion you. At age 12, through your imagination and inspiration, your Genius will take whatever you, or life, gives it to a higher level. That's why Waldorf Schools are such a robust base for life. Or *Genius* will help you resist the sometimes powerful, negative forces of the family forge of church, politics, or economics.

• • • •

KITES ARE ALL ABOUT capturing the tension between two dynamic sets of opposites in two bent sticks. Each of the two kite sticks is like a different aspect of our Genius. Both must be put under tension and bent into an arc and joined together ... they are necessary.

The vertical stick represents our upright self, which stands between the spiritual and the earthly poles. The horizontal stick represents that which goes between our self as an individual and the world.

The meeting changes depending on our age: teen, young adult, adult, or senior.

If you put too much pressure on any stick, it will crack. Sticks are rigid and fixed, bodies and psyches are more malleable.

In kite making, you have to risk having enough arc to generate lift. Adding tension in life is risky because Genius is both positive and negative; there is always the danger of unbridled egoism, hubris, anger or violence, or fear, depression, and brooding.

The sticks are bent to create a wing shape, and highflyers are the ones who can take what life gives them – positive or negative - and generate more than enough draft to create lift well more than the weight of their situation. It's a mix of wingspan, angle of the wing, and velocity of the wind.

Genius inspires all arts, transforms all effort into art, and all people into artists.

The configuration or the form of the art is the wingspan. For a writer, a haiku, for example, is a short, intense form with high imaginative velocity. Meaning, inspired in the reader, gives lift (or not). The angle of the message rises above culture and makes use of the headwinds. Genius inspires all the arts.

Genius is in all craft, all handwork, or earth focused and inspired as well – farmers, contractors, carpenters, mechanics, handwork teachers, or gardeners. We all have connections with the spirit and with our communities.

Kites can spin out of control if the *Genius* is too intense and one-sided. A kite can spin pointlessly in a strong headwind and won't rise unless there is a counterbalance. To handle a headwind, a kite, a *Genius*, requires a counterweight – a tail.

• • • •

KITE TAILS ARE BITS of fabric tied together and attached to the earthly end of the spirit/earth pole. Separate bits of life brought together. Each is a memory of failures, regrets, embarrassments, tragedies. Bike boat crashes. Gravity. These are what gives weight to our souls. We are glad they have sunk beneath our consciousness. They are not gone. But, when tied together, they seem so much.

Successful people have more than the average number of failures in their lives and are not afraid of failure. As Michael Jordan once said, "I have failed over and over and over again in my life – and that is why I succeed." (YOUTUBE Nike Commercial)

A wise highflyer with extraordinary Genius to see into the spiritual world, Rudolf Steiner, has said that when we die and look behind ourselves as we ascend into the spiritual world, that our egoism, failures, misdeeds, sins, and errors stream behind us like the tail on the kite of our Genius. They *are* the tail of the kite of our Genius. When we age, the tail grows and grows. What gives our loft, lessens.

The memorial services which I have attended for friends have a public portion in which we speak and honor the Genius of the dear-departed friend. And at the same time, we sit in unspoken silent remembrance of their flight, including the failures, misdeeds, and poor choices which have balanced their lives.

The headwind blows. Are we able to rise with it? Do we still struggle? Do we risk failure? Bike boats of middle-age? Are we still in contact with the source of the true, the good and holy of our Genius, which is a grace? What is the source of what holds us back, the failures, mistakes, and evil in our lives?

Stand in that headwind!

CITIUS – ALTIUS – FORTIUS

FASTER – HIGHER – STRONGER

This excerpt published originally in the author's
https://th3simplequestions.blogspot.com/
Essay category winner, 2017 AGELESS AUTHORS ANTHOLOGY

FROM NAÏVE IDEALISM TO ACHIEVED IDEALISM

WHO ARE YOU?

Naïve Idealism is falling in love with an ideal or a person or project that represents an ideal that takes your breath away, fills you with flaming enthusiasm, ideas, plans, dreams, and hopes for the future. At long last, you have THE IDEAL, a lofty, meaningful purpose. A Quest. An Impossible Dream. You imagine the difference you can make, the unique contributions *you* can offer, how *you* can be of service to *the* project, *your* team, *your* lover.

You have been waiting for this. Is this a destiny moment? Your life will be forever changed. You will make a significant gift, and in return, you will be enriched, your life will have greater meaning and importance. You can almost see the smiles on your loved one or the team. They KNOW what you have done. You can practically hear their appreciative remarks. Those who thought you didn't have the right stuff will, at long last, know your TRUE worth. YOU made the difference between success and failure - even under tremendous pressure.

WHY ARE YOU HERE?

Or they will break it to you – and usually not so gently. They will give you a dose of reality. Pour cold water on your enthusiasm. They've seen your head in the clouds. Heard your vanity. They take it upon themselves to pop your balloon. This is not about you, they say. You didn't have the whole picture, they opine. You didn't know the ropes, they gossip. You were NAÏVE – that's why it's called "Naïve Idealism."

It was somebody else's turf all along, and, unfortunately, you thought otherwise. How presumptuous! Where did you get THAT idea? Somebody else was in control. You were a newbie in a shark tank. Your lover had someone else. Somebody didn't give you what you needed to do it right. You were ill-informed. They should have told you before. Now you look like a fool. Feel embarrassed. The ideal is not yours alone. This is not the first time this has happened. Why does this always happen to you? Why do you still wind up with the short end of the stick, out of luck, with a bunch of losers who never liked you anyway?

Naïve Idealism (or Love 1.0) is a gift to everyone – you don't have to EARN it – and it will bring you a picture of what COULD have been – of your higher and better self – and then that free and easy type of Idealism shattered that picture. Whoever it was that designed all this[1] was very clever because you now face the three Horsemen of The Personal Apocalypse: Bitterness, Blame, and a Broken Heart. But before you ride one of those horses into the world - look around. You'll find that there lots of footprints out of that lonely place.

WHAT DO YOU WANT?

Rudolf Steiner, a 19th-century social scientist, introduced *Achieved Idealism* in a lecture called *"Awakening to Community*[2]*."* Steiner says that we are like dreamers who become conscious of our real capacities in this cage-match over Idealism. It is through others that we awake, and once we are awake, we have to work hard to achieve our ideals through our efforts. There are so many others who want to take ideals away from us, keep us feeling powerless, unfree.

Do you want the real deal? You want "Achieved Idealism"? You have to start with the steel of your courage. To make hardened steel, called "tempered steel," the Smith must heat it and pound it. To become wise, you must be "seasoned" by going through an entire spectrum of unwise actions leading to failure. To Love, you must love

---

[1] Fate, Destiny, or your Higher Self?

[2] Awakening to Community Lecture IX, by Rudolf Steiner, Dornach, March 3, 1923, https://wn.rsarchive.org/Lectures/AwakeComm/19230303p01.html

and be loved. Steiner says it is our community that helps us achieve our ideals and tests us personally - and we need both.

Pick an ideal – the bigger, the better – liberty, equality, altruism, religion, democracy, sobriety, chastity – change yourself? - your choice. Then set out to achieve it step by step. Take courage with you and look for others to support you or challenge you – makes no difference which. Every encounter is an opportunity to learn something about yourself, either positively or negatively. Then based on that feedback, make one small change. This leads to one more quality you need – tenacity.

Look at the poem which inspired Nelson Mandella as he sat in prison - *"Invictus"* - *"I thank whatever gods may be for my unconquerable soul."* [1]

Unconquerable - that's an ideal.

© Copyright 2014, Jean W. Yeager
All Rights Reserved

---

[1] INVICTUS – William Ernest Henley,
https://www.poemhunter.com/poem/invictus/

THE KITE OF YOUR GENIUS

I Am Your Nested System

Lend me your Higher Self for a moment, will ya?

• • • •

AUTHOR'S NOTE:
I am really sorry to have to bring this very complicated schema up at a time like this, I know you're busy; but I can tell some of you are struggling with weight loss, stopping smoking ("cessation" as it is called now), modifying a habit, parenting, dealing with aging parents, grumpy colleagues, or angry young people – then you simply must be aware of how this nested system works.

You might have heard of something that sounds a lot like this on Dr. Oz, but probably not correctly. I didn't make this stuff up by myself; I learned it. I cannot make any magic claims. This is an OPERATING HYPOTHESIS, PEOPLE – NOT DOGMA. Ready? Here we go.

• • • •

WHO AM I?
I am your nested system. We are Five Sheaths, which are nested within your physical body like a Russian "Babushka" doll.

The Physical Body is Sheath #1. In this definition, that physical body is the physical material that is left after you die.

If you're not dead yet, then the life or living part that animates your physical body is Sheath #2. This is called the "Life" Body. In some metaphysical constructs, it is called the "etheric" body. This includes our Sense Body or Sentient Body. It is comprised of our experiences with the world – physical and emotional – fight or flight, bumps, accidents, joys of success – things we sense, but these sensations come AFTER something happens. It's that place where "muscle memory" lives. It's the "Stuff Happens" body. But, when we get old enough to generate our thoughts, feelings, and emotions like love, hate, fear, attraction, these bits which we build up are added to this

Sentient Body. Beyond these two are containers that are less physically connected with the body.

Thoughts and feelings are experienced too, and this is then called the Psychological or Emotional Body. Also, in other metaphysical texts called the "Astral Body." So, that's Sheath #3 – it's all about consciousness – we dream in our feelings and are awake in our thinking.

The next sheath, Sheath #4, is called the Ego. Our Ego ... what do you say about the Ego? It seems there are two aspects of the Ego – a "lower self," the more self-centered or "egoistic" aspect which wishes a continually greater share of life's bounty and sees itself as the most important part of creation (as an attorney told my lower-self once – "all money flows toward you" – of course, my lower-self hired this attorney); and a "higher self," which we rarely show to others. This higher self is nourished by creativity and is that which can genuinely say "I." The higher self is influenced by our Spiritual Self.

And, Sheath #5, is our Spiritual Self. Our Spiritual Self lives in a world of ideals, inspiration, Angels, and also counter (negative) influences.

Okay. So this is the Nested System, which we all have.

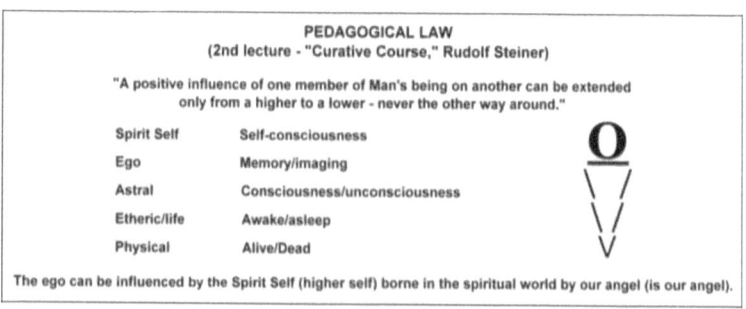

https://1.bp.blogspot.com/-uEnQxalx2L8/U2pAbiriy3I/AAAAAAAARc/Ml50d0EURWc/s1600/PEDAGOGI-CAL+LAW+v.3.jpg

WHY AM I HERE?

You're a Genius, right? And, smart people look good, right? So, you're here for weight loss, of course. Isn't that why you bought this book? Or maybe another habit change.

There is a law that governs all changes of habit in this type of "nested system." Rudolf Steiner called it the *"The Pedagogical Law*[1]*"* and it says that in such a nested system of sheaths the next "highest" sheath can influence the next "lowest" sheath.

So, to lose weight, my Spiritual Self, which lives in the world of the ideal and inspiration, gets inspired that my physical body should lose weight. My Spiritual Self goes to the Ego to get the team on board. My Ego can't simply say to my physical body, "I got an idea! We're gonna lose weight. Now!" or command the body: "Lose weight!" Nope. Won't work.

My Ego must work through the next lower sheath – my Emotional/Astral and say, "I know you love chocolate, éclairs, peanut brittle, etc. but Higher Self has been inspired to lose weight – so I'm not getting any more chocolate." Then the Emotional Body weeps, moans, and complains constantly but will eventually work with the Life Body and say, "I know you have a physical craving for sugar right now, but the team is working on losing weight. Let's do some walking, eh?" And, eventually, the Physical sheath will shed pounds.

In a nested sheath, you can't skip a step. Your Ego has to work its way through each sheath. Fairly unorthodox so far, eh? Maybe not today.

WHAT DO I WANT?

I want to let you in on a secret, so if you haven't bailed by how there is a REAL mystery piece here – something hidden.

---

[1] Rudolf Steiner, Lecture #2, *"Curative Education"*

The sheaths that are contained in our physical body are discreet to our body system. The other sheaths – Psychological / Emotional Body, Ego, Spiritual Self - are available to be extended to others.

As an example: An adult can use their Ego working through their Emotional Body to help calm an anxious child because your Ego development and strength is greater than theirs. Your Emotional Body can influence a child's Life Body – if you can soothe yourself, you can sooth them. Or, if you need to energize a youngster for an activity, you have to work from your enthusiasm.

One note from an old geezer - parents, PLEASE! It does no good to drag a wailing child through the mall and scream at the poor child: "Mind me!" because, at such a young age, the child doesn't have a "mind" or Intelligence yet! But, let me NOT fall into lower-self blaming. Rather, let my Higher Self say to your Ego, "Hey, you know, you should try skipping. Make a game out of exiting!"

© Copyright 2014, Jean W. Yeager
All Rights Reserved

You And William Shakespeare Dream Each Other

WHO AM I?

Writers are dreamers who gather imaginations and fantasies and bring them down to words. When the reader reads what I have written, you read and imagine or experience my dream – and so you dream along with me. You follow along with my thinking and my path through the fantasies to the imaginations.

So, as a writer, I must be aware that the reader and I share an intimate, sacred space. I must be faithful to the reader because you follow my imagination, my interior becomes your interior, my passions, your passions (even if only for a while.) I must be cautious about what I write because it is not only for my self-expression, but what I write goes into your soul.

It all begins with the writer's dream and the reader's willingness to dream along with him.

When William Shakespeare wrote sonnets to his lover, he was a writer gathering imaginations and fantasies and bringing them down to words on paper. Still, the words expressed an intimacy and knowledge of the lover not known to the ordinary reader. And, when his lover read his writing, she dreamt of his dream more secretly. She followed along with his thinking and his path through his intimate fantasies to the imaginations.

As a writer, Shakespeare was aware that the reader/lover, and he shared a more intensely intimate, sacred space. He was conscientious about what he wrote because the response was just as highly charged and evocative for his lover as it is for him – and only slightly less for we readers hundreds of years later.

WHY AM I HERE?

The reader or dreamer of the writer's dream has what may be called a Night Man Consciousness versus a Day Man Consciousness. The Day Man Consciousness begins when you wake in the morning and drag your emotions and body out of bed and ends when you go to sleep at night. The Day Man consciousness is sense-bound. When the Day Man lays down to rest, the body and energetic self, your Night Man, arises and unfolds. This is a deeper sleeping than the reader's sleep.

The Day Man believes that all of life is measured by its accomplishments – the stuff of your to-do list, what you post on Facebook and tuck into photo albums - the resumes, degrees, awards, milestones along the concentric circles of your life: business trips, family carpooling, smalltown worries, shopping, and Starbucks, culminating in a headstone.

The Day Man in space, the Night Man, exists in time. His/Her existence is measured in cycles of time, rhythmical patterns, seasonal revels, festivals, evolution, joy, warm welcomes, canning, gardens, growth, children, and all expressions of love. The Night reveals a world qualitatively different from the experience of the day.

Shakespeare's Sonnet XLIII is the dream in which the dreamer meets the lover in the night – this is dreamer writing the dream in which he describes the Dream Lover.

"When most I wink, then do mine eyes best see,
For all the day they view things unrespected;
But when I sleep, in dreams they look on thee,
And darkly bright, are bright in dark directed.
Then thou, whose shadow shadows doth make bright,
How would thy shadow's form, form happy show
To the clear day with thy much clearer light,
When to unseeing eyes thy shade shines so!
How would, I say, mine eyes be blessed made
By looking on thee in the living day,

> *When in dead night thy fair imperfect shade*
> *Through heavy sleep on sightless eyes doth stay!*
>> *All days are nights to see till I see thee,*
>> *And nights bright days when dreams do show thee me."*

When you now, hundreds of years after it was first written, re-read Shakespeare's dream of the Dream Lover, a mood of the night remains. A feeling perhaps. Not the stuff of Day Man Consciousness.

• • • •

WHAT DO I WANT?

We are all sleepers in the dreams of others. Before you were born, lofty spiritual beings dreamed you into existence. Where are they now? Who is dreaming the dream of you? Who is writing your story? Whose ideals or ideas fill your inner world? Where do you go when you sleep? With whom do you commune? Who is it that dreams that "deep and dreamless sleep" as silent stars go by over the Little Town of Bethlehem?

When, where and why will we awaken, lose our illusions or become disenchanted? As D.H. Lawrence writes in *"The Song of the Man Who Has Come Through,"*

> *"What is the knocking?*
> *What is the knocking at the door of the night?*
> *It is somebody wants to do us harm.*
> *No. No, it is the three strange angels*
> *Admit them, admit them."*

© Copyright 2014, Jean W. Yeager
All Rights Reserved

THE KITE OF YOUR GENIUS

I Am Your Crisis

WHO AM I?

I am the crisis that defines you. I may be that sudden automobile accident, that diagnosis, that unexpected email rejection. I can be as quick as a slap across the cheek. Or I may be one of those slow-moving crises that seem to eat away at your gut day after day. That step off the edge of the pond, you were two years old and went in over your head and gave you the fear of water for the rest of your life. That poker game in which you were suddenly in way over your head. I am the panicky business investment that you have made, and you're about to lose it all. The lie that came back to you. The little mistake that now has gotten out of control. That prescription which was going to ease the pain? Remember me? The Crisis took your beautiful watercolor painting and slopped indigo paint on it[1] - trailed it across your pretty bright colors. I am the splash of indigo in your life – your heart attack, your cancer, the abortion, the DUI, the Oxy addiction, the perfect relationship gone wrong. There go your plans. Your hopes! Your dreams! Shot to hell. Screwed. And you are left with what? Broken dreams? Broken idealism? You're left broken.

WHY AM I HERE?

I bring you choices you would never make for yourself. I come to you, and your higher self-offers your weaknesses up to me, just like Father Abraham. You are the son I must slay. I take you, and I break you so you can have a choice. I give you a choice, just like God gave Abraham that choice. I un-fix the fixed. I cause you to consider tightening up what's loosey-goosey. What will you do? Will you blot up the indigo paint on your pretty colors? Pretend I never happened? Will you give up? Cry over your broken dreams? Get corrective

---

[1] CRISIS painting exercise.

surgery? How will you hide a broken heart? Get 'tude? Look for a White Knight? (You know that indigo will never TOTALLY blot up! Everyone can tell. Everyone knows.) The memory will always be there.

Why were you broken? Was it something you did? Or something you ARE? Are you guilty? Have something to hide? Were you broken to let something OUT? Or to let something IN? Is the being broken the end of something else? Or is it only the beginning? How do you respond? How will your higher self-respond?

Everyone starts with "naïve idealism." But, once you're broken, you can create "achieved idealism" out of the ashes of your dreams that went down in flames. "Achieved idealism - the second marriage of you and your disillusioned self. It's discovery, recovery, learning, and the lesson. You're not a beautiful couple. A little indigo around the edges - imagine deep dark indigo mixing with the crimson, yellow and blue – new hues appearing stronger deeper more potent than you ever imagined. That's why I'm here. To create the new, improved, and damaged you.

WHAT DO I WANT?
I want to live, and love, in universal imperfection. Couch surf with your karmic carpool. I am in the limbless arms of another who holds you. I am the ravaged face. The blind eyes. The drooping stroke smile. The limp. The drooling happy friend. The 12 Step groups you attend. I bring the impossible together with the improbable. I want you with me. I want you never to forget me, and I want you to carry me in your heart ... right where Abraham was aiming the knife. Your Treasure Chest.

© Copyright 2014, Jean W. Yeager
All Rights Reserved

Let's Reverse Our Will, Shall We?

The Struggle for the New Faithfulness

WHO AM I?

I am the things which control you: I am the Saros (the Sun and Moon barycenter), which through the courtesy of the Suprachiasnatiuc Nucleus (SCN) of your cell links your body to the circadian rhythms of day/ night. I am the geography of where you live or work. I am the cultural system of your people, tribe, gang, clan, corporation, neighborhood, school, or workplace. I am the local, regional, and national economy. I am the political system – federal, state, and local. I am individuals who have power over you - your parents, family, friends, enemies, whether they be naturally connected, blended by relationship or karmic carpool. These are some of the exogenous (outer) systems which control you.

I am also your endogenous drivers – your age and phase of development, place in birth order, body limitations (weaknesses, strengths), the addictive substances from the world which control you. I am your DNA, your biology, and your medical history. I am your inner personality fragments that drive you psychologically: compulsions, fears, doubts, anxieties, repulsions, attractions, habits, temperaments, memories, syndromes, dreams, chemical reactions to pharma, and psychological manifestations.

And then there is your spiritual dimension, how open you are to spiritual influences, your religious shaping, your destiny which somehow filters your perceptions or is a type of oscillator to excite you about some things and turn you off on others?

Our age is quite pleased with itself that it has so defined the human being in such intimate details.

WHY AM I HERE?

All these things which control us, define us to one another. They offer easy labels by which we can categorize one another with our quick scientific minds. Then, we think we "know" one another. And, because we have this modern thinking orientation which prefers simple categorization, in this time-pressured era, we sum each other up in simple phrases: little boy, old man, working mom, heart breaker, wise guy, or any of a dozen more. They are the stereotype, the shorthand picture.

When you meet me, when I meet you, we must work very hard to find one another amid all of the baggage which we carry – the complexity of who we are. Within all of these dynamics are the genuine you and the actual me.

One of the tricks for actually meeting one another is to reverse our wills. When we sit together, I say to myself; this is not about me; it is about you – I am here to serve you. What do you need? What's up with those piercings? And I can grow curious about you. The bigger space I can create within myself, and if I sit quietly and ask simple, straightforward questions, out of that very dynamic person you are, out of that complicated baggage and history, a unique person may emerge – even just for a moment.

WHAT DO I WANT?

I want that we try to tame one another and offer a space for that very unique other to feel safe enough to emerge out from within the complexities of themselves. To TAME one another – like the fox in *"The Little Prince."*

"To me, you are still nothing more than a little boy who is just like a hundred thousand other little boys. And I do not need you. And you, on your part, have no need of me. To you, I am nothing more than a fox like a hundred thousand other foxes. But if you tame me, then we shall need each other. To me, you will be unique in all the world. To you, I shall be unique in all the world ..." — Antoine de Saint-Exupéry[1], *The Little Prince*[2]

Meeting or taming is the first step toward a new FAITHFULNESS which Rudolf Steiner describes:

> *Make for yourself a new and strongly courageous view of Faithfulness.*
>
> *What is usually called Faithfulness passes so quickly.*
>
> *Let this be your Faithfulness.*
>
> *You will experience moments – fleeting moments – with the other person, when he will appear to you as if filled, irradiated, with the true essence of his Spirit. And then there may be – indeed there will be – moments, long periods of time when he becomes dried up and darkened. But you will learn to say to yourself at such times, "The Spirit makes me strong. I remember the true being of this person. I saw it once. No illusion, no deception shall rob me of it."*
>
> *Battle always for the image that you saw. The struggle is Faithfulness, and in this struggle, one person shall be near another, as if endowed with the Guardian forces of the Angels.*

© Copyright 2014, Jean W. Yeager
All Rights Reserved

---

[1]. *https://www.goodreads.com/author/show/1020792.Antoine_de_Saint_Exup_ry*

[2]. *https://www.goodreads.com/work/quotes/2180358*

THE KITE OF YOUR GENIUS

Age 28-30: The Wiser Person Within Us

WHO AM I?

The Wiser Person within us watches while we are riding the wave of our 20's – a time during which we feel we can do ANYTHING. This feeling is real because, for many, the early 20s maybe under the influences of others: parents, family, school, sports, or other activities surrounding natural abilities with which we have been born and in which we are encouraged to pursue.

By about age 28, many people reach the limit of this world. We can feel these capacities begin to diminish – or we grow jaded, and we sense we need a new direction in which to grow. This is when the Wiser Person within us brings situational limitations or our shortcomings to meet the demands of our future destiny to help us prepare and change.

In many biographies, this prompts a crisis that happens at about age 28, which is called THE CRISIS OF TALENT. Will we find a source of renewal of our "gifts" and natural abilities from the past? Or do we feel compelled – even driven - to break out and attempt to change ourselves radically?

WHAT DO I WANT?

When I was 28, I had spent many years in printing/publishing. But I had a dream of becoming a writer. My Wiser Person within used my boss as my "excuse" for me to quit and prompt my CRISIS OF TALENT. My wife was working, and so she agreed to support us for one year while I "became a writer."

My crisis deepened because the Wiser Person within me knew that I would fail - it was impossible to become a professional writer in one year! But he helped me confirm the truth of the world. I tried. I wrote a novel; I wrote a screenplay. I wrote for the neighborhood and alternative newspapers. But I wrote nothing for which anyone would pay me. It was clear after my year, I would not be able to earn a living as a writer, and I was too proud to go back to the midnight shift at the print shop. My wife and the Wiser Person within me said: "Go get a job."

Then the "Wiser Person" within me helped me realize that it wasn't the writing craft that needed all the attention; it was the BEING ME that needed to change. (Uh-oh!)

WHY AM I HERE?

After the CRISIS OF TALENT, a more profound phase shift may be necessary, as it was in my case. I would never achieve the outer goal of being a successful writer unless I changed inwardly, (a bit) dealt with my pride, my anger, and gained *some* humility; and social skills while polishing my natural writing skills. And more.

On the inside, it is like the seed of what you wish to become has been planted. But the seed of your future lies within the hard shell of who you are. In my case, I had done a great job of building up this cynical, stubborn, arrogant guy. All this had to be dissolved before the "new and improved me" could emerge and take root. That dissolving is painful but necessary to allow the future to sprout.

In my case, being humbled was solvent for my hardened ego. I took any job I could to meet the responsibilities of a family (midnight shift loading trucks). Once I began to soften, I noticed my wife and some of her friends were seeking a spiritual "path." Was I even aware there was a path? No. I had all the answers there, too. So, the Wiser Person woke me up to lots of things which were hardened into answers. The Wiser Person opened an inner space that became filled with questions: Was there something more that I ought to strive for beyond a profession (what I "profess" or say I want to be)? Was there, in any sense, a "calling" – something coming from outside leading me into the future?

The more I changed, the more it was possible for me to change, and the more the Wiser Person within me was able to lead.

How was Age 28-30 in your life? Did you experience a CRISIS OF TALENT?

> © Copyright 2014, Jean W. Yeager
> All Rights Reserved

THE KITE OF YOUR GENIUS

Remix Of Rudolf Steiner's Lecture "Facing Karma"

A REMIX OF WISDOM FROM

the past and the present – contemporary lyrics adding a dimension to the through-line message of Steiner's lecture.

EXCERPTS FROM: "Facing Karma" a lecture by Rudolf Steiner given in Vienna, on the 8th of February 1912, GA 130 The specific paragraph quoted is numbered at the end of the segment. See:
https://wn.rudolfsteinerelib.org/Lectures/FacKar_index.html

LYRICS BY: Paul Simon, Bob Marley, Bob Dylan, The Band, Eric Clapton ("Cream"), The Beatles, The Wallflowers. Bruce Springsteen, and Tom Petty.

THE BOY IN THE BUBBLE – PAUL SIMON
https://www.paulsimon.com/us/music/paul-simons-concert-park-august-15-1991/boy-bubble
"The Boy In The Bubble"

> It was a slow day
> And the sun was beating
> On the soldiers by the side of the road
> There was a bright light
> A shattering of shopwindows
> The bomb in the baby carriage
> Was wired to the radio
> These are the days of miracle and wonder
> This is the long-distance call
> The way the camera follows us in slo-mo
> The way we look to us all

The way we look to a distant constellation
That's dying in a corner of the sky
These are the days of miracle and wonder
And don't cry baby don't cry Don't cry.

RUDOLF STEINER:

> Why do we need comfort, consolation in life? Because we may be sad about a number of events, or because we suffer as a result of pains that afflict us. It is natural that, at first, man reacts to pain as though he is rebelling inwardly against it. He wonders why he has to stand pain. "Why am I afflicted by this pain? Why is life not arranged for me in such a way that I don't suffer pain, that I am content?" These questions can only be answered satisfactorily on the basis of true knowledge concerning the nature of human karma, of human destiny. Why do we suffer in the world? We refer here to outer as well as to inner sufferings that arise in our psychic organization and leave us unfulfilled. Why are we met by such experiences that leave us unsatisfied? (6)

= =

REDEMPTION SONG – BOB MARLEY
https://www.azlyrics.com/lyrics/bobmarley/redemptionsong.html
"Redemption Song"

> Old pirates, yes, they rob I;
> Sold I to the merchant ships,
> Minutes after they took I
> From the bottomless pit.
> But my hand was made strong
> By the hand of the Almighty.
> We forward in this generation
> Triumphantly.
> Won't you help to sing

These songs of freedom?
'Cause all I ever have:
Redemption songs;
Redemption songs.

RUDOLF STEINER:
By far the greater part of our pain and suffering is sought by imperfections that we have brought over from previous incarnations. Since we have these imperfections within ourselves, there is a wiser man in us than we ourselves are who chooses the road to pain and suffering. (9)

= =

GOTTA SERVE SOMEBODY – BOB DYLAN
https://www.azlyrics.com/lyrics/bobdylan/gottaservesome-body.htm
"Gotta Serve Somebody"

You may be an ambassador to England or France
You may like to gamble, you might like to dance
You may be the heavyweight champion of the world
You may be a socialite with a long string of pearls.
But you're gonna have to serve somebody, yes indeed
You're gonna have to serve somebody,
It may be the devil or it may be the Lord
But you're gonna have to serve somebody.

RUDOLF STEINER:
It is, indeed, one of the golden rules of life that we all carry in us a wiser man than we ourselves are, a much wiser man. The one to whom we say, "I," in ordinary life is less wise. If it was left to this less wise person in us to make a choice between pain and joy, he would undoubtedly choose the road toward joy. But the wiser man is the one who reigns in the depth of our unconscious and who remains inaccessible to ordinary consciousness. (9A)

= =

THE WEIGHT – THE BAND
https://www.azlyrics.com/lyrics/band/theweight.html
"The Weight"

> I pulled into Nazareth, was feelin' about half past dead
> I just need some place where I can lay my head
> "Hey, mister, can you tell me where a man might find a bed?"
> He just grinned and shook my hand, "no" was all he said
> Take a load off, Fanny
> Take a load for free
> Take a load off, Fanny
> And (and) (and) you put the load right on me
> (You put the load right on me)

RUDOLF STEINER:

> He directs our gaze away from easy enjoyment and kindles in us a magic power that seeks the road of pain without our really knowing it. But what is meant by the words: Without really knowing it? They mean that the wiser man in us prevails over the less wise one. He always acts in such a way that our shortcomings are guided to our pains and he makes us suffer because with every inner and outer suffering we eliminate one of our faults and become transformed into something better. (9b)

= =

CROSSROADS – ERIC CLAPTON /. CREAM
https://www.azlyrics.com/lyrics/cream/crossroads.html
"Crossroads"

> I went down to the crossroads, fell down on my knees.
> Down to the crossroads, fell down on my knees.
> Asked the Lord above for mercy, "Save me if you please."

I went down to the crossroads, tried to flag a ride.
Down to the crossroads, tried to flag a ride.
Nobody seemed to know me, everybody passed me by.

RUDOLF STEINER:
Little is accomplished if one tries to understand these words theoretically. Much more can be gained when one creates sacred moments in life during which one is willing to use all one's energy in an effort to fill one's soul with the living content of such words. Ordinary life, with all its work, pressure, commotion and duties provides little chance to do so. In this setting, it is not always possible to silence the less wise man in us. But when we create a sacred moment in life, short as it may be, then we can say, "I will put aside the transitory effects of life; I will view my sufferings in such a way that I feel how the wise man in me has been attracted by them with a magic power. (10)

= =

YESTERDAY – THE BEATLES
https://www.azlyrics.com/lyrics/beatles/yesterday.html
"Yesterday"

Yesterday,
All my troubles seemed so far away.
Now it looks as though they're here to stay.
Oh, I believe in yesterday.
Suddenly,
I'm not half the man I used to be.
There's a shadow hanging over me.
Oh, yesterday came suddenly.
Why she had to go
I don't know she wouldn't say.
I said something wrong,
Now I long for yesterday.

RUDOLF STEINER:

> We may now move on to another step in our experience. The anthroposophist should be determined to take this other step only after he has comforted himself many times with regard to his sufferings in the way just described. The experience that may now be added consists of looking at one's joys and at everything that has occurred in life in the way of happiness. He who can face destiny without bias and as though he had himself wanted his sufferings, will find himself confronted by a strange reaction when he looks at his joy and happiness. He cannot face them in the same way that he faced his sufferings. It is easy to see how one can find comfort in suffering. He who does not believe this only has to expose himself to the experience. (11)

= =

ONE HEADLIGHT – THE WALLFLOWERS
https://www.azlyrics.com/lyrics/wallflowers/oneheadlight.html
"One Headlight"

> So long ago, I don't remember when
> That's when they say I lost my only friend
> Well they said she died easy of a broken heart disease
> As I listened through the cemetery trees
> I seen the sun comin' up at the funeral at dawn
> The long broken arm of human law
> Now it always seemed such a waste
> She always had a pretty face
> So I wondered how she hung around this place
> [chorus:]
> Hey, come on try a little
> Nothing is forever
> There's got to be something better than
> In the middle
> But me & Cinderella

We put it all together
We can drive it home
With one headlight

RUDOLF STEINER:
While our pain and suffering lead us to ourselves and make us more genuinely ourselves, we develop through joy and happiness, provided that we consider them as grace, a feeling that one can only describe as being blissfully embedded in the divine forces and powers of the world. Here the only justified attitude toward happiness and joy is one of gratitude. Nobody will understand joy and happiness in the intimate hours of self-knowledge when he ascribes them to his karma. If he involves karma, he commits an error that is liable to weaken and paralyze the spiritual in him. Every thought to the effect that joy and happiness are deserved actually weakens and paralyzes us. This may be a hard fact to understand because everyone who admits that his pain is inflicted upon himself by his own individuality would obviously expect to be his own master also with regard to joy and happiness. But a simple look at life can teach us that joy and happiness have an extinguishing power. Nowhere is this extinguishing effect of joy and happiness better described than in Goethe's[1] Faust in the words, "And thus I stagger from desire to pleasure. And in pleasure I am parched with desire." Simple reflection upon the influence of personal enjoyment shows that inherent in it is something that makes us stagger and blots out our true being. (13)

= =

---

[1] .https://wn.elib.com/Bio/Goethe.html

GLORY DAYS – BRUCE SPRINGSTEEN
https://www.azlyrics.com/lyrics/brucespringsteen/glorydays.html
"Glory Days"

> I had a friend was a big baseball player
> Back in high school
> He could throw that speedball by you
> Make you look like a fool boy
> Saw him the other night at this roadside bar
> I was walking in, he was walking out
> We went back inside sat down had a few drinks
> But all he kept talking about was
> [Chorus:]
> Glory days well they'll pass you by
> Glory days in the wink of a young girl's eye
> Glory days, glory days"

RUDOLF STEINER:

> But inasmuch as we experience pain and suffering, we must recognize what man has made of the world during its evolution, which originally was a good world, and what he must contribute toward its betterment by educating himself to bear pain with purpose and energy.

= =

WON'T BACK DOWN – TOM PETTY
https://www.azlyrics.com/lyrics/tompettyandtheheartbreakers/iwontbackdown.html
"I Won't Back Down"

> Well, I won't back down, no I won't back down
> You could stand me up at the gates of hell
> But I won't back down
> Gonna stand my ground, won't be turned around
> And I'll keep this world from draggin' me down
> Gonna stand my ground and I won't back down

[Chorus:]
Hey baby, there ain't no easy way out
Hey I will stand my ground
And I won't back down"

= =

EPILOGUE:

Clearly this is a "generational" version. If you have interest in creating another version, let me know at:

<u>3simplequestions@gmail.com</u>

and I will see if we can get it posted. – Jean Yeager.

> © Copyright 2014, Jean W. Yeager
> All Rights Reserved
> All Lyric excerpts © Copyright the authors.

THE KITE OF YOUR GENIUS

Devotion Becomes Sacrifice

NOTE: THE CALENDAR Of Virtues is a year-long practice of looking into the world and into yourself to see if what Steiner says about our soul being visible in the outer world is, in fact, the case. This is a post for March 21 – April 20, 2014. One looks for Virtue Transitions or Opposites.

WHO AM I?

I am the Seed. I am all about Devotion. In me, I have bound together all of the genetic matter required to reproduce my species. My qualities have been gathered over successive generations of plants. Some have stayed, others have fallen away over time. And I can protect this special cargo for a very long time. Because I am a plant seed, I have enclosed the germplasm in a very hard seed-case.

Human Devotion is a virtue and gains strength when one spends time with something or someone important to you- including your plans and dreams. Like the seed, a practice of Devotion is an active gathering together all the knowledge, insight, and experience possible within yourself – and this can take time, lots of it.

WHY AM I HERE?

Sacrifice. The Seed is all about Devotion AND Sacrifice. When the time is right, I have got to be able to transform myself – to sacrifice one form - the form I am most comfortable with, have spent so much time perfecting - to become another – sacrifice my beautiful hard-shell to become reborn as a plant. I'm gonna need some help. When I'm planted in the dark earth and broken down by water, warmth, and life in the soil, that to which I have been devoted, will be released. Without Sacrifice, the "new and improved me" cannot be re-born.

Self-sacrifice is uncomfortable. Sometimes if you are in the midst of personal change it can actually feel as if something within you is dissolving; something hard or fixed is breaking down.

THE OPPOSITE: Not Caring

The Virtues of Devotion and Sacrifice depend upon Care. There is a risk that they can draw you into a type of hyper-devotion, dogmatism, or fanaticism. To guard against these excesses, many may develop a negative virtue of distancing themselves by not caring or cynicism. The sole soul question is how to stay objective but devoted and engaged. How to come close without merging.

WHAT DO I WANT?

The questions I ask myself are: Has Devotion been easy? Hard? Has it gotten stuck? And how is it going with your self-transformation? Is it time to practice the Virtue of Sacrifice and give up that to which we are devoted so that something new can come into the world, and into yourself?

© Copyright 2014, Jean W. Yeager
All Rights Reserved

The Substance Of Love

WHO AM I?

When I was growing up – maybe three years old - my family lived next door to an older, "widow woman" whom I called "Auntie Helen" who had a bushy head of salt and pepper hair, who wore thick glasses, chain-smoked and laughed a deep, rumbly smoker's laugh. She wasn't really my Aunt, but in those days, all the women on the block of tiny houses in our wannabe prosperous neighborhood in San Antonio were my Aunts, and all had full permission to act like my mother when my mother wasn't around.

Many times I would go to Auntie Helen's house, and the first thing she would ask is, "Have you eaten? Are you hungry?" and I would nearly always say, "No, I haven't eaten, and yes, I am hungry."

So, Auntie Helen would cackle and prepare my favorite: Uncle Ben's "Instance" Rice with a big pat of butter. I remember Auntie Helen used a white enamel pan to boil the water, and my mother didn't. I wondered if that was a magic pan that made her Instance rice taste better. It wasn't the rice that was special; it was what Auntie Helen put IN the rice – Love. Auntie Helen transformed the Instance rice into the Substance of Love.

WHY AM I HERE?

Bees are a community of Love. A hive is like a "being." Individuals all selflessly devoted to gathering pollen in an incredibly intimate fashion: parting the petals of the flower blossoms, crawling inside and licking, sucking, and licking the dust. The bee then travels to another plant, and in that intimate visit, it pollinates that plant. Each hive is devoted to Love and helping the flowers make Love.

Imagine the hundreds of bees that live in each hive going out each day to make Love to dozens if not thousands of plants in a considerable diameter around their hive. That's an incredible, invisible community task without which the flowers, fruits, and plants in a large area cannot grow. They cannot pollinate themselves. I remember a Vacation Bible School song, which goes, "Bees, Bees of Paradise, do the work of Jesus Christ. Do the work that no man can."

When the community of bees return to the hive each day, they have a second intimate task: they transform the pollen into honey and propolis with which to feed the Queen and bee babies. Honey then, is made by a community devoted to Love in order to serve the community. Rudolf Steiner called Honey the "Substance of Love" and asks us to recall the inner experience of the taste of honey on our tongue. He says this is an experience of Love. We all need to experience Love.

WHAT DO I WANT?

Our world is going through a time where there are fewer resources. Consequently, people may individually feel "needy" for themselves but are abundant resources for one another – their community.

Volunteering is better than bowling alone. I once spent several years teaching self-development courses as a volunteer in maximum security prisons. The men and I met as equals, and we talked about life. I presented a few straightforward but very challenging exercises from Rudolf Steiner that are called "The Six Subsidiary Exercises." I'm not sure whose "self" was developed more – theirs or mine?

So, if you do volunteer at your church, hospital, Boys and Girls club, weeding at a community farm, busing tables at a Food Kitchen. Everybody can do something. Even calling an elderly neighbor and reminding them to take their medicine is an Act of Service – an Act of Love.

Hunger of many types – physical and emotional is on the rise in our communities – become an Auntie Helen for someone else, transform your pan of Instance Rice into the Substance of Love.

THE KITE OF YOUR GENIUS

Selecting Omens

WHO AM I?

I am an omen. You do not know who I am because you have not been taught about omens. Once all school children could recognize indications, or impending actions because they had read in Holy writ about omens, which were integral to life as the ancient people knew it. These are things at which you now scoff.

Omens were and ARE signs for your future. We portended what will become. We are not created by men to point to things men cannot imagine. We are not the "coming soon" signs. We are world-happenings, like eclipses, earthquakes, the darkening of the sun or moon, asteroids, falling off mountains, death of species created by the world-creator.

There once were people who could experience our signs and explain their meaning – what they portended. And, once dreams could be interpreted.

Now, "learned" people can see no future, relegate dreams to personal psychic disturbances, experience no Angels, believe that "global anything" beyond science can't be real, and discount things so significant as superstition. Is this in itself an omen?

WHY AM I HERE?

You are always presented with omens. All around you are "signs of the times," which you may ignore or not. You may only be aware of small omens for your personal life. Can you even extend your gaze wide enough to see the generational portents, national omens, international omens?

When you expand your gaze wide enough to include as much as you can, you may have felt feelings that arise: joy, gratitude, connection, concern, even fear or doubt. Consider a particular part of your world, of THE world, and note the feelings which arise. These are your intuitive feelings about that part of life. You may even become aware of a specific "trigger" for these feelings. What does the future look like for this part of your life?

In this way, you participate in the world's becoming. You de-isolate yourself. You may be able to connect in new ways with the world.

WHAT DO I WANT?

The development or evolution of our consciousness has left us as "observers" and disconnected from the spiritual world. In many ways, the spiritual world relies on humans to be responsible for life.

The omens are given to us so that people may remember to "turn to an ancient principle" – "matter is never without spirit."

Here is an ancient Rosicrucian verse from Rudolf Steiner (1861-1925):

> *"Seek the truly practical material life but seek it so that it does not numb you to the spirit which is active in it. Seek the spirit, but seek it not in passion for the supersensible, out of supersensible egoism, but seek it so that you wish to apply it selflessly in the practical life in the practical world. Turn to the ancient principle, matter is never without spirit and spirit is never without matter, in such a way that we say we will do all material things in the light of the spirit and we will so to seek the light of the spirit, so that it evokes warmth for us in our practical activities."*
>
> —*Rudolf Steiner*

© Copyright 2014, Jean W. Yeager
All Rights Reserved

Report Of Teaching Rudolf Steiner's: "Six Subsidiary Exercises" To Jail Inmates In Rutland, Vermont 2015

Dear Readers -
Sorry to break the form of the blog but I wanted to share this with you.
—Jean

BACKGROUND:

- "A Call to Arms on a Vermont Heroin Epidemic" [1] – NEW YORK TIMES, February 27, 2014
- "The New Face of Heroin"[2] ROLLING STONE, April 3, 2014
- "Vermont Tackles Heroin Addiction: Progress measured In Baby Steps" [3] –NEW YORK TIMES, February 25, 2015

• • • •

IN FEBRUARY 2014, THE *New York Times* and regional television news channels unofficially dubbed Rutland, Vermont (my hometown), the "heroin capital" of the U.S. Like many areas, loss of jobs, bad economic times, and other social factors, made our area easy prey to dealers. This was not news to us who were residents of Rutland, but we were shocked to learn how bad it was. We were naïve and "asleep."

---

[1]. http://www.nytimes.com/2014/02/28/us/a-call-to-arms-on-a-vermont-heroin-epidemic.html
[2]. http://www.rollingstone.com/culture/news/the-new-face-of-heroin-20140403
[3]. http://www.nytimes.com/2015/02/26/us/as-vermont-tackles-heroin-addiction-progress-ismeasured-in-baby-steps.html?_r=0

My son, who moved in with my wife and me, that February asked me if I knew what was really going on with frequent, short stops by cars at my neighbor's house. I had to admit I didn't know." My son, who had joined us after his own "rough patch" at age 29 who lived for months in a ghetto in Florida, informed me that it was a good bet that the boy next door was selling drugs. I was stunned. He was not an isolated case.

Within a year, the community reacted to this apparent epidemic. It began a large-scale effort of police, city policy wonks (housing), everyday citizens, businesspeople, and mental-health workers to attempt to change the dynamics within the community. A project "Vision" was launched, which is still underway today six years later. I have been a volunteer in this effort since it was launched. Everyone has been encouraged to get involved in *any* way.

SIX EXERCISES – EIGHT WEEKS

We moved to Vermont from Michigan several years ago. Before I moved to Vermont, when I lived in Michigan, I taught an 8-week introduction to Steiner's "*Six Supplementary Exercises*[1]" to inmates in maximum security prisons. After I moved, I proposed to offer this program at our local jail in Rutland, the Marble Valley Correctional Institution (MVCI). I use the pamphlet, "*Self-Development In The Penitentiary*" by Fred Janney, Board Chair of the Anthroposophic Prison Outreach (APO) program sponsored by the Anthroposophical Society in America.

This time I was to incorporate material from David Kahneman's book, "*Thinking, Fast and Slow.*[2]" Kahneman put important scientific

---

[1] SIX STEPS IN SELF-DEVELOPMENT *The Supplementary Exercises*, Rudolf Steiner, Selected by Ates Baydur, Rudolf Steiner Press, 2010

[2] THINKING, FAST AND SLOW, Daniel Kahneman, Farrar Strauss and Giroux, NY, 2011

research "wheels" under Steiner's exercises in that Kahneman articulated two systems within the human psyche: System 1 (S1) an "automatic system" for thinking, feeling, and willing. S1 is our automatic "set-up" practices about which we are mostly unaware. And the research identified System 2 (S2) an "effortful" system by which we challenge our in-built, automatic system. Steiner's exercises are all about moving from S1 behavior to S2.

Steiner offers something Kahneman doesn't – specific exercises for S2 thinking, S2 intentions, and S2 feelings, S2 openness, S2 positivity.

The exercises represent the kind of an "architecture," which gives inmates meaningful experiences of change in *being* different – no matter how briefly. The six exercises are like spokes on a wheel that revolve around a central hub of *personal integrity* – a subject of much conversation – how to have a chance to change and rebuild a life.

The architecture was identified by the late John Davy in his book *Hope, Evolution and Change*[1] many years ago when he compared the six exercises to Kűbler-Ross' steps to recovery in *Death and Dying*: denial requires new thinking, anger is a rebellion of the will, bargaining requires equanimity, depression is healed with positivity, acceptance needs openness and hope comes from harmony. Certainly, the men incarcerated will go through these steps at some time, consciously or not.

Jail is different from prison. In prison, men are incarcerated for years. In jail, weeks, or months. I had 25 inmates over the eight weeks. Five of those completed all eight weeks and were given a "certificate" of completion which may have value in their parole process. The ages were as young as the 20s and as old as the 50s. Most crimes were non-violent. The weeks were:

---

[1] HOPE EVOLUTION AND CHANGE, John Davy, Hawthorne Press, 1990

(1) *Introductions / Overview*, "Rules of The Road"

(2) *Control of Thinking* – practice in concentration, focus thinking, overcoming "flighty" thoughts, distraction, and finding an undisturbed period.

(3) *Control of Intentions* – mastery of impulses, regularity, accomplishment.

(4) *Control of Feelings* – tolerance, forbearance, equilibrium, and equanimity.

(5) *Positivity* – looking for the good, the true, and the beautiful in each situation. (The guys said to me, "Are you kidding, Jean? We're in *JAIL*!" So, I replied: "Okay – what's your option? Look for the bad (evil), the false, and the ugly? Lots of that around here. Your choice.)

(6) *Open-mindedness* – the ability to not let the past dictate the future, staying flexible, meeting other minds.

(7) *Harmony / Balance* – repetition of exercises.

(8) *Maintenance* - Creating choice architecture that controls S1.

The weekly sessions became opportunities for men to discuss the experience of incarceration and how to make choices to improve their experiences – inside and out of jail. Shared problem solving emerged regarding all sorts of issues: recovery, dysfunctional family dynamics ("That teenager just pushes my buttons!"), and internal jail pressures were handled within Steiner's framework.

Following the 8-weeks, I conduced a follow-on 4-weeks of "Communication Skills," which added listening, questioning, and presentation skill-building. Written evaluations of the 8-week program were provided to Jail Administration, and we intend to repeat the program on an ongoing basis.

I encourage each of you to get involved where you live. By teaching these very simple exercises, we get to practice them again and again, and some of us (me) need that. Are they really "supplementary"? "Supplementary" to what? These *ARE* the exercises.

Jean Yeager. Rutland, Vermont

© Copyright 2014, Jean W. Yeager
All Rights Reserved

SHE COAXES THE HUMAN SPIRIT

WHO IS SHE?

She is an MD, a therapist, a mother, but in the pre-scientific era, she would have been the Hermit in her cave or the Wise Woman in front of the fire. Today the fire into which she gazes is a medical records computer screen. She is the Oracle who consults her techno-runes, the bones, the stars, the history, the lab results, her notes, and her heart. She turns her Prophetic Gaze inward on herself and recalls the patient's rattling chest, the general strength or weakness, fever, and clammy touch ...? She sees each prior check-up and looks into her mind's eye and sees us, her patients, in detail. She fields a call from her daughter and discusses their dinner plans. Then, she adjusts herself inwardly and comes to the exam room.

WHY IS SHE HERE?

She walks through offices, ERs, waiting rooms, quiet or noisy, dressed in her white lab coat. She pauses at the doorknob to the exam room and rallies her weariness into a sense organ, which she will focus on the patient. There is nothing that passes this good woman's eye. Nothing too trivial for her to consider. She will take in each of us and compare it mentally with her inner review – our last visit - looking for changes. In this wounded world, the quiet power of her eye and her stern gaze gives comfort to the frightened, courage to the dying, and careful attention to the Willy Lomans who whine and carp about declining forces, failure, or change.

WHAT DOES SHE WANT?

In her childhood days, she coaxed frogs into jars and yellow perch onto hooks. Her patients, too, are wild things and shy. Some put on brave faces. Others seek sympathy. Some angrily deny their fate. The exam room reeks of regret. Holding powerful emotions and great science on some unseen scale of destiny, she seeks to coax the human spirit in each patient into full flame. She starts with small, simple, innocent questions, "How are you today?" and waits, listening. Agonizingly, slowly she can hear the heart creaking open, or if the human thing is unable to arrive, she is prepared to retire in hope, pain, fear, or grief in her solitude.

© Copyright 2014, Jean W. Yeager
All Rights Reserved

Arduous — Beschwerlich Ardu — И Взрывоопасных —مشکل

WHO AM I?

I hope that this is an arduous time for you. Arduous, or "tough" times mean you are being challenged and tested by life.

How much "grit" do you have? Grit is comprised of determination, willingness to withstand the pain. To call forth determination or courage means that you are willing to sacrifice for your goal.

Big goals call forth significant challenges.

That means you are rising to the challenges by growing, learning, gaining experiences. The more difficult the experience, the harder you have to work. The harder you work, the greater the capacities you develop. The more exceptional capabilities, the more you can accomplish and achieve. That means your life can become more abundant. The more abundant your outer life becomes, the more inner strength you have.

WHY AM I HERE?

The challenges we receive lead us to the fate we have for our life. That fate and those experiences are directed by the star our spirit self has chosen to follow.

Is it you who is finding your fate, or is your fate finding you?

Is it your star which you are following? Or, is the star leading you, drawing you forward into the future you know nothing about?

As you move forward on your path, you may begin to realize that we must have challenges, a path, fate and a star, otherwise, our struggles seem random and meaningless.

WHAT DO I WANT?

What is the gift we receive? We receive the giver.

Who is the giver?

As the Rudolf Steiner verse reads:

> *"I feel my star,*
> *My star finds me,*
> *I feel my fate,*
> *My fate finds me.*
> *My life and the wide world are one.*
> *Life grows more abundant for me.*
> *Life grows more radiant within me.*
> *Life grows more arduous for me."*

This is a time of testing.

Why in the world would anyone want their lives to be more arduous?

> © Copyright 2014, Jean W. Yeager
> All Rights Reserved

WHO LET THE DOGS OUT?

WHO AM I?

I keep three big dogs, and I keep them fenced in. I keep them for self-protection. Sometimes they get out and run about terrorizing people. And I have to go chasing them. Then I have to apologize. These are very BIG dogs, and they make a big difference in my life. I could not do without them. I do my best to try to hold them in, but BIG dogs can seem like they have a mind of their own.

The first dog is ANGER, the loudest barking dog of the bunch. But he helps keep away BAD people. What would I do without Anger? He is probably the most aggressive of all three.

My second dog is DOUBT. I can't tell if he is around unless I hear him grumbling. He sits in a corner, sniffs stranger's trousers, and shakes his head. Mostly he growls. But I gotta say, Doubt can be aggressive too.

My third dog is EGOISM. I'm so Proud of him! He is just everything that I've ever wanted in a dog! Yeah, when my Ego gets out and starts running around everybody better get out of the way!

Whup! There they go! I always wonder *who* lets those dogs out?

WHY AM I HERE?

Well, I gotta chase down those dogs for one thing.

And I'm working on dog training. If that fence is not gonna hold 'em, then I better be responsible for where those puppies run.

Dog training means you have to be smarter, kinder and more action oriented than your dogs. That means you have to train yourself – change yourself. Discover why you let your dogs be so ill-behaved.

What do you need to do to be in control of your big dogs?

WHAT DO I WANT?

People are always asking me, "Why do you keep a dog like Anger, anyway? Why don't you just get rid of it?" You don't want to get rid of your Anger, do you? I think you just want Anger to transform into Love.

That way, Anger will lead you to Righteous Indignation and won't cower if it comes across an even bigger dog like Hatred.

I'm training Doubt to sniff out the Truth. When Doubt does sniff at trousers and shaking his head, that just means this person's got something I don't understand. That means I got to spend time learning their Truth.

And Egoism? Well, I want that puppy to lead me to the people who are bigger dogs – really big "Alpha Dogs" - so that I can learn Humility and if they have the "real juice," I want to learn Reverence.

Who let the dogs out? Maybe the Wiser Person within me?

© Copyright 2014, Jean W. Yeager
All Rights Reserved

I Am Dis-Incarnation: Age 42, The Hinge Year

WHO AM I?

I am disincarnation – the gradual grapevine step that you make as you dance your way off the stage of life. I've been in the script for years – you're only just now beginning to notice my entrance. Perhaps it was the wrinkles? Maybe a little arthritis around the edges? Some hair loss, mmm? And the menopause ads seem more present.

Your vitality and health, which for all these years lived deep in your skeleton, is now packing up and going to Florida. All your hormonal doodads are beginning to pack their bags, too. They know that you are watching the commercials, which suggest that their sell-by date is approaching. They will be replaced by hormonal treatments as offered by the young, the virile, and the buxom sales team on the telly. Truthfully, with the exception of big-time pharma for men with E.D., this is the same stuff that's been offered since the late 1800s to generation after generation with similar results. You do age. You will die. Still spending money and applying creams will give you and me something to do and pass the time while you disincarnate!

WHY AM I HERE?

Ah, but this is an EXCITING time! Age 42 is THE hinge year. You may feel, "It's too late!" or "I'm getting bogged down." Or, strangely liberated. At age 42, you can look into the windshield of your life and see the off-ramp for death. And out the rearview mirror - your birth and childhood waving "bye-bye!" This is like the autumnal equinox of your life where the future and past are in balance. Some say it feels as if you have a moment of weightlessness – where all forces are equal, which can be frightening. Others say that you can feel the most enormous sense of freedom and potential.

Age 42 is the year in many biographies in which breakthroughs and radical shifts of all kinds have taken place: Galileo made his first telescopic discoveries, Freud published *"Studies on Hysteria,"* it was Jung's most critical period, Betty Fridan published *The Feminine Mystique*, and Rosa Parks chose to stay seated.

WHAT DO I WANT?

This "mountain top" experience is a great time to look at your life. Your child-rearing years may be behind you, but now is the time for "spiritual children." And a new type of seeing may be possible – an inner vision may bring you "insights," which you will learn to trust.

But now is the time for you to make serious plans and do research on how you will spend your life after age 62 – the next great hinge!

To re-phrase an old saying that says:

"From age 21 to age 42 we try many things and learn how to live.

From age 42 to age 63, we learn to sort through what we have lived and choose what we love.

From age 63 to death, we live only what we love."

© Copyright 2014, Jean W. Yeager
All Rights Reserved

Pinball Age

WHO AM I?

I have been rolling downhill on my old-style, electro-mechanical pinball life. I bounced from bumper-to-bumper, location-to-location, job-to-job, crisis-to-crisis, and person-to-person. Did I control any of this, or did I only control my desire-flippers at the bottom?

I am now propelled by the gravity of aging and the inertia of my vanities. I now realize that I am unable to alter the linear direction of my descent toward "Game Over," which prior events have orchestrated. Even the speed of my fall is cumulative. My rolling silver steel ball of personality appears out of my control. I watch all that is going on behind the glass game-top and wonder if I have become a "deaf, dumb blind kid" like *Tommy*.

Can't I choose anything? Do anything?

Then again, do I want to choose? Or should I simply let the events choose? That's the easiest. Less effort, right? Watch my little steel ball go straight down and disappear out of sight. Then I can curse "what they did to me," those stupid bumpers. Blame someone else for my fate, my lack of opportunities — the lack of wealth of my parents, genetics that gave me an "eecch" brain. Maybe whine about the obviously rigged game of life which is *not* on the level. Oh sure, there were inclinations, mine on the inner, and the inclined game table on the outer. And, after all, I chose this game.

And I was inclined to try to affect the outcome. I shook the table, nudged it – *hard* (careful not to "tilt"). But basically, a pinball life is three balls, flashing lights, sounds, points rolling on the board as you stand there somewhat confused, unaware, naïve, numb in my heart and alone. Yeah, I flipped my desire flippers and occasionally kept the ball in play.

Choose. Huh? Yeah, right.

WHAT DO I WANT?

Let me brood in my dull anger for a moment, okay?

Do I want to choose? Yes, I *do* want to choose. And I realize that if I choose, then I will pay for my choice. I will suffer. I *do* suffer. Your extra replays don't come free. But I'm brooding already, right? I have a few more games racked up on the counter – a few more years before "*Game Over.*"

Deprivation because when you choose, you only get one thing – not both. I have to pick one or the other, poverty, because I can't have both (or the many). There will be labor, conflict, looming fear, addiction (to my desiring. Desiring? Hell. Longing!), regret that things will not be harmonious, rejected divinity, failing physical capacities, pissing myself. Maybe denial is easier. Just let me stand here like *Tommy* – deaf, dumb, and blind. But *Tommy* could play. Am I a player?

Suffering. Suffering to be me. A warrior, a player, chooses to define her/himself from the others. Can I be hostile? Independent? Push back against the inclined table of life? I *can* be hostile to the amorphous, undefined!

I long for the One Thing. The One Thing we have in our hearts, our True Self. The others told me that *real* success was getting my steel ball into the 1,000 Points Hole. Roll your ball into that Hole and score big time, lots of lights, sounds, and chatter. Woo-hoo! ("You get a replay!") And, then the 1,000 Points Hole ejects you, shoots you across the table.

That other thing which warms your heart? That True Love? Where is that? Don't seek that. There is no choice, they say. Stick with the 1,000 Point Hole and replays. You are what you are, the game is the game, the table is what it is, and that is that. True Self? True Love? Not here. Not in this game. This is a closed system. There is no place to go for that.

WHY AM I HERE?

I am here to awaken the True Self before I die before you die.

"Time, time, time, see what's become of me ..." I am a child of the 60s in my 60s. What time is it? Am I late for a very important date? *"When the Moon is in the 7th House ..."* Is this the dawning? Have I missed it? When was that Millennium? Y2K?

Is it ever too late to transform? If you don't transform yourself, life will transform you. So, you have to go from the closed system to an open system.

If I am a steel ball, I am iron. Iron is malleable with enough heat. With enough passion, I will undergo the agony of change. I will stand between the opposites where I'm normally *not* inclined to go and feel the power of resistance. Resistance to my passion cranks up the heat. With enough passion, resistance, and friction, I can change. Form a blade. A sword. The One Thing to become my new self. Someone who does not just roll mindlessly, who can overcome the inertia of the past. A blade does not roll mindlessly. A blade cuts you away from the amorphous, which clings. Change - the one precious thing to do - the act which grows more fierce with each sunrise.

True Self awakens in the sphere of cause. Outside the box. Off the table. Choose to be the gravity, your self-motive. This is how we roll.

© Copyright 2014, Jean W. Yeager
All Rights Reserved

CALL TO ACTION

The kite of your genius lifts your community the genius of communities lifts our society.

1) A FREE REVIEW COPY eBook is being sent to Leaders in the communities listed below with a request that they review this book. If you would like one, just email:
   luckyphonecall@gmail.com,
   and I will send you a code to use on eJunkie for a free review copy.

2) I hope you will write and publish a review of this book on your organization's newsletter or web site. If you do, please let me know where the report is published, and I will send your organization a code for your members to take $1 off future eBook purchases.

3) It would help me if you were to re-publish your review on my Goodreads Author Profile Page:
   https://www.goodreads.com/author/show/13734788.Jean_W_Yeager

4) I hope this book has made you curious about the broader community of organizations or advocates for which you may have an affinity - here is where you can find out more – this is the CALL TO ACTION! A further step.

5) Your visit and engagement with any of the listed organizations gives lift to their spirits! Check them out! They would appreciate your visit.

THE KITE OF YOUR GENIUS

About The Author
Jean W. Yeager

Award-Winning Essayist, Playwright, Prison Volunteer, Waldorf Dad, Quaker, Former Administrative Director of The Anthroposophical Society in America

CONTACT: 38 Kendall Ave., Rutland, VT 05701
jwyeager2@gmail.com

INTERNET REFERENCES:

Professional background site: https://www.the-three.com/

Linkedin: https://www.linkedin.com/in/jeanyeager2/

Blog - Three Simple Questions
https://www.threesimplequestions.blogspot.com/

NPX (NEW PLAY EXCHANGE)
https://newplayexchange.org/users/23580/jean-yeager

Collected advertising scripts, speeches, films and commercials accepted into John W. Hartman Center for Sales, Advertising Marketing History in the U.S.

Duke University Libraries:
https://library.duke.edu/rubenstein/findingaids/yeagerjean/

RECENT WRITING AWARDS / PLAY PRODUCTIONS:

2024 – Indy Script Selected - *"Prisoner #101067 Public Speaking Report: The Life and Times of Tupac Shakur And Excerpts From The Prince by Niccolo Machiavelli"* by Indy Black Filmmakers Association of Houston Festival.

2024 – Produced - "Iraq War Prayer: Photo-Op", Rogue Theatre Festival, Fresno, CA

2022 – Finalist, 3rd Place, Tennessee Williams and New Orleans Literary Festival One Act Competition, , *"Prisoner #101067 Public Speaking Report: The Life And Times of Tupac Shakur And Excerpts From The Prince by Niccolo Machiavelli"*.

2020 – Winner, Ageless Authors National Creative Fiction Contest, *"Old Pirates of the Heart."*

2019, Finalist, Ageless Authors National Essay Contest, *"That Ol' Certainty!"*

2018 Wrote / Directed "Clothesline" for the Dorset, VT One-Act Play Festival

2017, Winner *Dead Mule Southern Writers* – Memoir Category – "The Invisibles Are Back"

2016, Winner, Ageless Authors National Essay Contest, Dallas, TX - "Kite Justice"

2016, Finalist, Tennessee Williams National One-Act Contest, New Orleans, LA - *"How Santa Claus Came To Zone Whisky Alpha Romeo"*

RELEVANT EXPERIENCE:

1967-1970 – B.A. English Literature, Colorado State University (CSU).

1970-1971 – Radio Television Film, CSU, Post-grad studies

1972-1978 Editor of Regional Editions, *The United Methodist Reporter,* Dallas, TX.

1978-1982 Stanford Agency, the in-house ad agency for The Southland Corporation, the parent company for 7-Eleven and other companies.

1982-1989 – Jean W. Yeager Creative Services Award-winning copywriter/speechwriter.

1989-1991 – Research, Teach and Consult in Organizational Development (OD) at The Centre For Social Development, Emerson College, Sussex, U.K.

1991-1996 – Change Consultant, Envision Associates, Spring Valley, NY.

1992-1994 – Managing Editor, *BIODYNAMICS* Journal

1996-2006 – Administrative Director, The Anthroposophical Society in America.

1998-Present: Teaching in Maximum Security Prisons self-development programs: Introduction To Biography (Phases and Stages) and Six Subsidiary Exercises.

2007-2010 – Centre for Anthroposophy, taught Biography (Phase Development Theory) to Waldorf faculty around the country.

OTHER BOOKS BY JEAN W. YEAGER

Fire Borne:
Anthroposophy in America

FIRE BORNE tells the story of the Anthroposophical Society, a small spiritual group inspired by Rudolf Steiner (1861-1925), and "daughter movements," like Waldorf Education, Biodynamics, RSF Social Finance, Arts, Camphill Villages, Medical/Therapeutic Centers, Publishers, etc. This book is a timeline, starting in 1886, that shows not only the major and minor happenings within the Anthroposophical Movement, but also what was happening at that same time throughout the World. This timeline is a richly illustrated history of the results of the work which this small group achieved in fighting the culture wars over its first century in America. **2023 Anthroposophical Publications**

Th3 Simple Questions:
Slice Open Everyday Life

Th3 Simple Questions are not answers, they are the tools by which we can probe deeply into our life, love, loss, family, and culture. I focused the questions like a lens on a different part of my life, turned the lens slightly, and was surprised by what appeared. This book is an invitation to try it yourself. Use the three simple questions: "Who Am I?", "Why Am I Here?" and "What Do I Want?" as prompts for journaling and deep reflection. At the core of faith are questions, not answers. The Spirit that forms the answers forms the one that answers the questions as well. **2015, Westbow Press**

www.ingramcontent.com/pod-product-compliance
Lightning Source LLC
Chambersburg PA
CBHW030532080526
44586CB00011B/413